THE MAGNIFICENT
BOOK OF
MICROSCOPIC
CREATURES

THE MAGNIFICENT BOOK OF MICROSCOPIC CREATURES

ILLUSTRATED BY
Isabel Aracama, Fede Combi,
Mat Edwards and Val Walerczuk

WRITTEN BY
Anne Rooney

weldon**owen**

Written by Anne Rooney
Illustrated by Isabel Aracama, Fede Combi, Mat Edwards and Val Walerczuk

weldon**owen**
Copyright © Weldon Owen International, L.P. 2024

All rights reserved. No part of this publication may be reproduced, distributed, or transmitted in any form or by any means, including photocopying, recording, or other electronic or mechanical methods, without the prior written permission of the publisher, except in the case of brief quotations embodied in critical reviews and certain other noncommercial uses permitted by copyright law.

Published by Weldon Owen Children's Books
An imprint of Weldon Owen International, L.P.
A subsidiary of Insight International, L.P.
PO Box 3088
San Rafael, CA 94912
www.insighteditions.com

Weldon Owen Children's Books:
Designer: Claire Cater
Editor: George Maudsley
Consultants: Dr. Jeroen Ingels, Dr. Alejandra Perotti, and Dr. William Foster

Weldon Owen would like to thank the following for permission to use their images as art references: María Teresa Aguado and Arne Nygren via *PLoS One*, María Herranz, Andy Murray, Chim Chee Kong, Reinhardt Møbjerg Kristensen, Rogelio Moreno, Diego Fontaneto, and Robin Smith. Weldon Owen would also like to credit the following for the use of their images as art references: Gilles San Martin (head louse, varroa mite, needle midge), Brian Valentine (chalcid wasp), Oliver-C (weevil), Katja Schulz (hemispherical scale insect), Patrick Clement (pygmy sorrel moth), Alexander Wild (pharaoh ant) and Hajime Watanabe (water flea). With special thanks to Dr. Łukasz Kaczmarek, Dr. Vanessa L. Knutson and Professor Timothy Barraclough for their expert advice.

Insight Editions:
CEO: Raoul Goff
Senior Production Manager: Greg Steffen

ISBN: 979-8-88674-069-1

Manufactured in China.
First printing, November 2024. RRD1124
10 9 8 7 6 5 4 3 2 1

Introduction

We live in a world of large animals—of people, cats, dogs, horses, birds, pigs, and lions. But within this is another world, one teeming with microscopic life. It is a vast realm of tiny creatures that outnumber larger animals by millions, and it includes some of the strangest animals imaginable.

These tiny animals live all around us, in soil, seawater, lakes, and rivers, unnoticed until we take out a microscope or magnifying glass. Every cubic meter of soil or water is usually packed with hundreds of thousands of miniature living things. They are essential to the functioning of life on Earth, clearing up waste and feeding larger animals, yet they often live their extraordinary lives unseen.

The Magnificent Book of Microscopic Creatures takes you on a voyage through the microscope, deep into the domain of the secret creatures that lurk around us. Meet an animal that can survive being frozen for decades and a mite that lives in your eyelashes. See a slug that hides a shell under its patterned body and the bug that feeds on your blood. Find out about a dragon that lives in the mud, a wasp that lays its eggs inside other creatures' bodies, and an arachnid that controls pests in your home. Discover the sea creature that can survive in space—so small that 20 can fit on top of a pencil eraser.

Travel down to the magnificent world of the minute as you get to know the tiny creatures that live unseen alongside us.

Fact file

Lives: Worldwide

Habitat: Fresh water, wet soil, damp moss, seawater

Size: 0.2–0.5 mm long

Eats: Decaying organic matter, algae

Contents

Dust mite	8	Bryozoan	30
Polychaete	10	Bedbug	32
Head louse	12	Chalcid wasp	34
Mud dragon	14	Peacock mite	36
Tardigrade	16	Weevil	38
Springtail	18	Loriciferan	40
Tanaid	20	Hemispherical scale insect	42
Sheep tick	22	Follicular mite	44
Varroa mite	24	Slender herald snail	46
Black bean aphid	26	Needle midge	48
Pseudoscorpion	28		

Flatworm	50	Fruit fly	66
Oribatid mite	52	Bdelloid rotifer	68
Nematode	54	Cat flea	70
Copepod	56	Head shield slug	72
European red mite	58	Ostracod	74
Pygmy sorrel moth	60	Red velvet mite	76
Pharaoh ant	62	Water flea	78
Scabies mite	64		

Dust mite

Dermatophagoides sp.

- Dust mites hide in soft furniture, bedding, carpets, and rugs in people's homes. They feed on the flakes of skin that fall off humans and pets.

- All mites are arthropods—invertebrates, or animals without backbones, that have legs with a number of joints and an external skeleton that covers and protects a body made up of segments, or connected parts.

- The feces, or poop, of a dust mite can cause allergic reactions in humans. Mites can also trigger the symptoms of asthma.

- A dust mite's body is not clearly divided into different parts like other animals. It is difficult to tell where its mouthpart ends and where its body begins.

- The mite's feet are absorbent, allowing them to stick to a surface and hold many times the creature's own body weight.

- These mites live for up to three months.

Fact file

Lives: Worldwide
Habitat: Bedding, furniture
Size: 0.1–0.4 mm long
Eats: Dead skill cells, mold

An adult human sheds about ¼ to ½ ounce (0.7 to 2 grams) of dead skin each day—enough to feed 1 million dust mites!

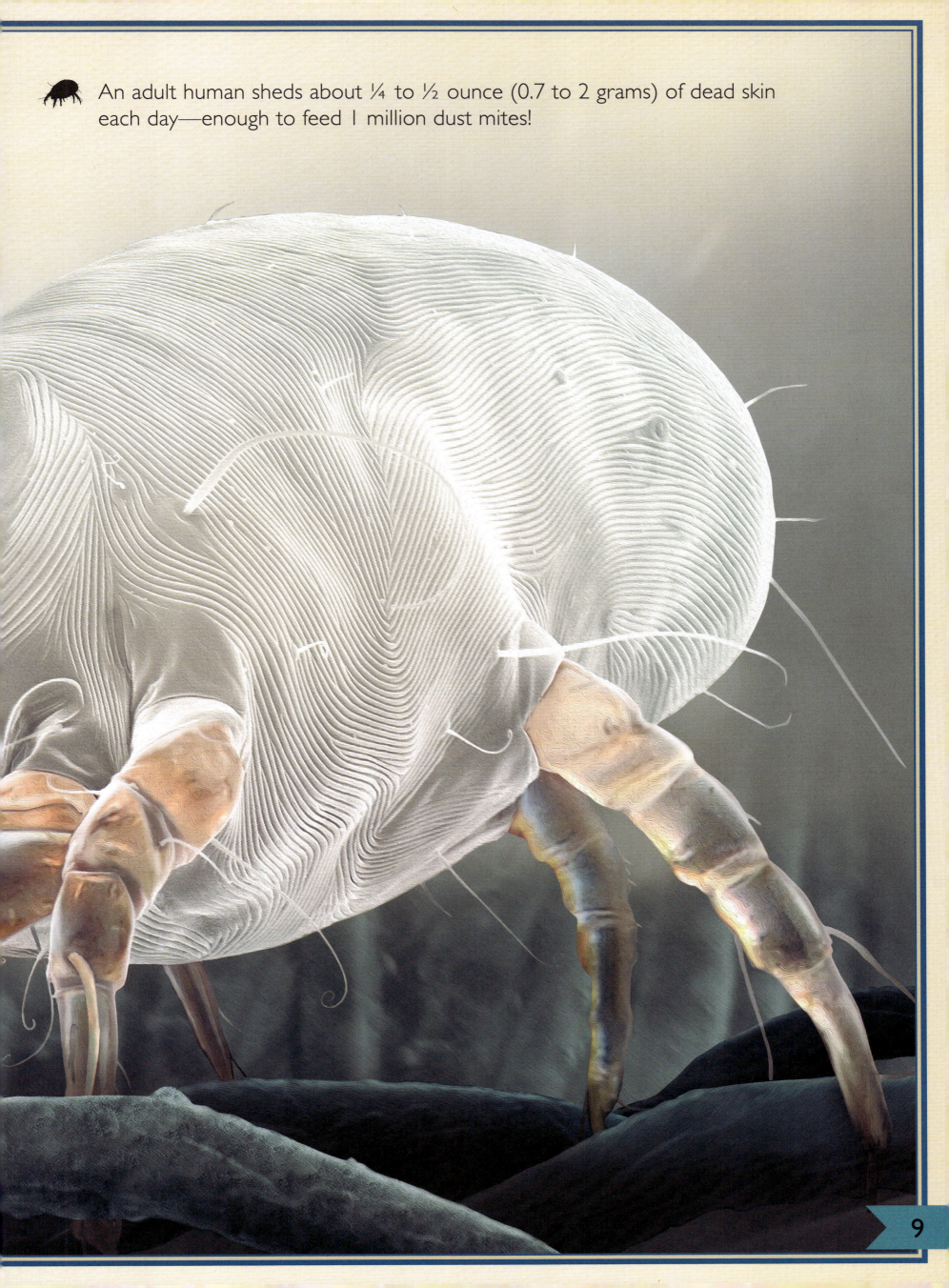

Polychaete

Amblyosyllis sp.

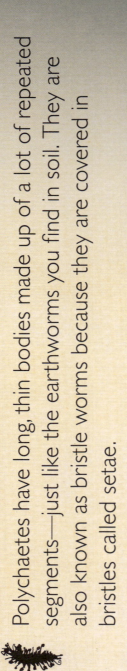

Polychaetes have long, thin bodies made up of a lot of repeated segments—just like the earthworms you find in soil. They are also known as bristle worms because they are covered in bristles called setae.

This polychaete is a species of Amblyosyllis worm. These creatures have long armlike "limbs" called cirri, which are often curled into spirals. The cirri can be longer than the worm's body.

The worms have a ring of six to eight teeth in a circular mouth, and up to four red eyes. They also have sensors to detect chemicals present in the water.

Polychaetes move using their bristles and a type of small foot called a parapodia. Each polychaete segment has a pair of parapodia sticking out.

When the worms are ready to reproduce, they swim away from the seabed and spawn in the open water.

Some types of polychaete produce a separate, short worm from their rear end just to reproduce! After growth, the new worm breaks away and floats to the sea surface, releasing its eggs.

Fact file

Lives: Worldwide
Habitat: Coastal waters
Size: Up to 5 mm long
Eats: Sponges; other food unknown

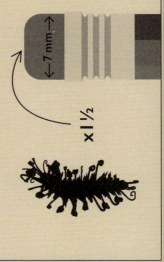

Head louse

Pediculus humanus capitis

- These little creatures are parasites—organisms that live on another species. They can be seen with the naked eye living among the hairs on people's heads and feeding on blood from the scalp.

- A female head louse lays six to 10 eggs a day, and about 100 over her lifetime.

- Female lice make a sticky substance to glue their brown eggs to the shaft of a hair near the scalp. The eggs hatch after six to nine days, leaving behind the yellowy-white empty cases, known as nits.

- Head louse hatchlings are called nymphs. They look like tiny versions of the adults. The nymphs mature into adults in seven days and begin to feed on blood.

- At the end of each of the head louse's six legs are hooks. These grasp hairs and make the louse hard to remove.

- Head lice inject a chemical into their host to stop the blood thickening so that they can drink for longer. The lice feed several times a day.

Fact file

Lives: Worldwide
Habitat: Human head
Size: 2–3 mm long
Eats: Blood

Head lice live up to 30 days but die after one or two days if they are not on a host they can feed from.

Mud dragon

Echinoderes sp.

- Mud dragons are tiny wormlike creatures that live in the sand or mud of the seabed. They get their name from their dragonlike appearance under a microscope.

- The mud dragon has a head, neck, and trunk, or body. The trunk is divided into 11 segments in adults, but fewer in young mud dragons. The segments are covered in protective plates that move as the animal moves.

- Many marine creatures release thousands of eggs at once. Scientists think the female mud dragon mates only once in her lifetime and produces just one fertilized egg at a time. She builds a package of mud around the egg to keep it safe until it hatches.

- This animal can withdraw its head completely into its body, covering the opening with hard plates on its neck. It is a bit like a turtle hiding its head in its shell!

Fact file

Lives: Worldwide

Habitat: Seabed, shorelines

Size: Up to 1 mm long

Eats: Microscopic algae, bacteria, organic debris

The mud dragon does not have limbs to help it move through its muddy home. Instead, it reaches forward with the rings of spines around its head and clamps them into the ground. It then pulls its body up to meet the head. The creature inches along by extending and contracting its body.

Tardigrade

Macrobiotus sp.

- These tiny creatures are the great survivors. They can endure extremely harsh conditions, including pressure six times greater than that at the bottom of the ocean, temperatures from -521°F to 302°F (-272°C to 150°C), and the dangerous radiation of outer space.

- Tardigrades live in damp places and are often found in moss. They must keep a thin layer of water around themselves so they can breathe. They live anywhere they can stay moist, from sand dunes to coasts, mountaintops, the Antarctic, and the deep sea.

- Each of their eight feet usually has two to four claws, but can have up to 12. They help the creatures grip as they move around.

- The tardigrade's body is covered by a hard cuticle, a bit like a grasshopper's. To grow, the tardigrade sheds its skin and hardens a new one.

- These animals have survived being stored in a freezer without food for 30 years and being fired out of a high-speed gun at 1,000 yards (900 m) per second.

- If there is too little or no water, tardigrades dry up into a ball called a tun until things improve. The tun can be just one hundredth the size of the tardigrade.

Fact file

Lives: Worldwide
Habitat: Damp places
Size: 0.5 mm long
Eats: Plant matter, microorganisms

←7 mm→

×14

Springtail

Dicyrtomina ornata

- These creatures are known as springtails because of their furcula, a forked, tail-like part folded under the body. When the furcula is released, it slaps the ground, springing the animal into the air with great force.

- This type of springtail is one of the Symphypleona (*sim-fy-plee-oh-nuh*) order. These animals all have very round bodies and long antennae.

- When faced with a predator, a springtail can make a sudden leap to safety in just milliseconds. To the attacker, it is like the springtail suddenly disappears.

- Some springtails can leap up to 100 times their body length. That is like a human child jumping higher than the Statue of Liberty.

- Natural antifreeze in their bodies means some springtails can even live in such cold places as Antarctica and Greenland without freezing.

Fact file

Lives: Worldwide

Habitat: Soil

Size: 0.2–3 mm long

Eats: Decaying plants, fungi, algae

- 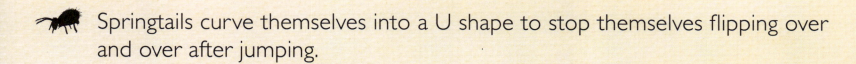 Springtails curve themselves into a U shape to stop themselves flipping over and over after jumping.

- 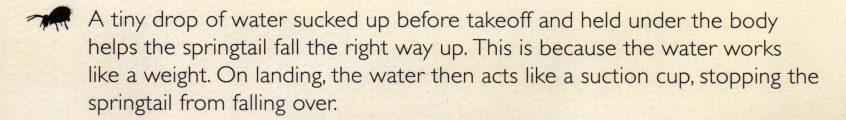 A tiny drop of water sucked up before takeoff and held under the body helps the springtail fall the right way up. This is because the water works like a weight. On landing, the water then acts like a suction cup, stopping the springtail from falling over.

-  Some springtails live close together. There can be up to 100,000 in just a square yard (1 square meter) of ground.

Tanaid

Sinelobus sp.

- Tanaids are tiny crustaceans that look like long shrimps with very short legs. There are at least 1,500 different tanaid species, and possibly as many as 55,000.

- This tanaid is a *Sinelobus* species. It lives on muddy seashores around Singapore. Other tanaid species live worldwide. They can be found in small tubes they make by burrowing into the mud or sand in order to hide themselves.

- These creatures live in all sorts of watery habitats. They are found in the deep ocean abyss, salt lakes, hydrothermal vents, and even underwater mud volcanoes.

Fact file

Lives: Singapore
Habitat: Muddy seashores
Size: 2–3 mm long
Eats: Unknown (this species); tiny organic remains (other species)

x3 ←7 mm→

- Along with some other shrimplike animals, tanaids have six pairs of walking legs at the front of the body, and usually have a few pairs of swimming legs toward the back.

- Many tanaids including *Sinelobus* have very large front claws. The claws are usually larger on males than on females.

- Females lay eggs that they carry in a pouch on their body called a marsupium. The eggs hatch in the marsupium but remain there for a while as they grow.

- A tanaid egg hatches not into a larva, or young, but into a manca. The manca looks similar to the adult but cannot swim well. Mancae stay near their mother, and large populations grow in a small area. In some places, up to 100,000 tanaids can be found in 1 square yard (1 square meter) of seafloor.

Sheep tick

Ixodes ricinus

- Ticks are usually flat when they have not fed. But this tick is so full with an animal's blood that its body has become hugely swollen. A tick can get three or four times longer by feeding.

- The sheep tick is a parasite—it lives and feeds on other animals. It can be found drinking the blood of a number of large mammals, including sheep, horses, dogs, and deer.

- These ticks live for two to four years and feed on three different animals in this time. Their journey starts as eggs laid on the ground, which hatch into larvae. These live on insect-eating animals, such as moles or hedgehogs.

- Sheep ticks have no eyes. They "see" using a special organ called a Haller's organ. It uses smell to help the tick understand its surroundings.

Fact file

Lives: Europe, North Africa
Habitat: Large mammals
Size: 2.4–3.6 mm long
Eats: Blood

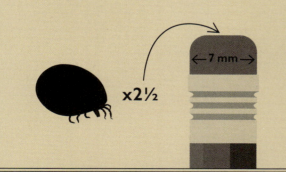

- Young sheep ticks have been found on more than 16 species of bird.
- Sheep ticks can also bite humans, and carry many diseases dangerous to people and animals.

Varroa mite

Varroa destructor

- These mites are parasites. They live on Western and Asian honeybees.

- Female varroa creep into honeycomb cells in a beehive to lay their eggs. This is where bee larvae grow. The mites make sure they are inside before the bees seal the cells, ready for the bee larva to turn into a pupa, or cocoon, and finally an adult bee.

- Varroa mites are the largest known ectoparasites, or parasites that live on the outside of their host, compared to the size of the host animal.

- These mites hide under the liquid food left in a bee's cell for the bee larva. They use breathing tubes called peretrimes to survive while in the liquid.

- When a bee larva has eaten the food stored for it in its cell, it becomes a pupa, the next stage in its life cycle. The female varroa living there bites a hole in the pupa to feed. When her several eggs hatch, the nymphs also feed on the larva through the hole she has made.

- Bad mite infestations can lead to the death of colonies, or organized populations, of bees.

Fact file

Lives: Europe, Asia, North and South America, parts of Africa
Habitat: Bee bodies, beehives
Size: 1.8 mm long, 2 mm wide
Eats: Honeybee body tissue

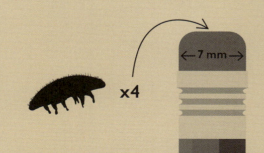

- Male varroa mites hatch in sealed bee honeycomb cells, mate with females, and die there. The females leave the cell when the bee reaches adulthood and breaks through the seal. The mites crawl onto adult bees to catch a ride as the bees fly around. They can move to other bees or even between hives.

- The female varroa mite's flattened shape allows it to slip between the body segments of the bee it is on. Here, the mite bites into the soft tissue to feed. Her claws and special hairs keep her attached to the bee.

Black bean aphid

Aphis fabae

 Black bean aphids, or blackfly, live on soft-stemmed plants. They pierce stems and leaves with needlelike mouthparts to suck the plant's sap. They do this so slowly that it can take up to 24 hours to begin feeding.

 Aphid eggs hatch in early spring on woody shrubs. They are all wingless females. In May, winged females are born. These fly to softer plants, including beans. Here, further generations are born as live young, including males. In late summer, aphids return to the winter shrubs to mate and lay eggs.

 Female aphids can reproduce alone, giving birth to live young. Each female lives about 50 days and can produce 30 young.

 Winged aphids are produced to help with overcrowding on their plant homes. Their wings allow them to leave for new host plants, easing the overcrowding.

Fact file

Lives: Warm areas of Europe, North and South America, Asia, Africa

Habitat: Soft shoots and leaves

Size: 1–3 mm long

Eats: Sap from plants

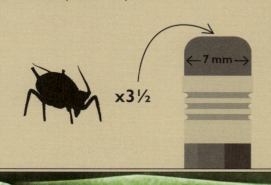

Two tubes, or siphunculi, at the animal's back end produce a waxy liquid. The aphid can pour this over an attacker in self-defense.

 Aphids are born pregnant—the next generation is already growing inside a newly hatched aphid, and the generation after that is also already there inside the developing embryos. That is three generations in one!

Pseudoscorpion

Pseudoscorpiones sp.

- The pseudoscorpion might look like a scorpion, but it is not a scorpion at all. Both creatures are in fact different types of arachnid, like spiders.

- Unlike a scorpion, a pseudoscorpion does not have a curved tail with a sting at the end. Instead, its weapons are two long, poisonous pincers, or pedipalps.

- One type of pseudoscorpion called the book scorpion is often found in houses. It eats book lice, dust mites, and the larvae of clothes moths. Its diet helps keep places free of these pests!

- This creature's venomous pincers paralyze tiny insects and other arthropods. The pseudoscorpion then uses its digestive juices to dissolve its prey, before chewing it and finally sucking in the remains.

- Some pseudoscorpions weave silk cocoons, or cases. They live in the cocoons over the winter or hide in them while shedding their skin during the next stage of their development.

Fact file

Lives: Worldwide

Habitat: Decaying vegetation in woodland, grassland, sand dunes or salt marshes; nests and burrows of other animals; houses

Size: 2–8 mm long

Eats: Arthropods

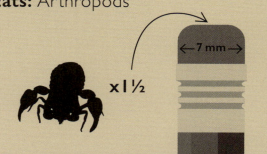

Female pseudoscorpions carry fertilized eggs in pouches attached to their bodies. The young hatch in the pouch and take in a milklike substance the mother produces from her ovaries.

Bryozoan

Cristatella mucedo

 Bryozoans are tiny water animals that live together in colonies. There are thousands of different species found in both fresh water and seawater.

 These bryozoans are *Cristatella mucedo*. Like other bryozoans, this species forms worm-shaped colonies up to 4 inches (10 cm) long in rivers and lakes.

 These creatures are nicknamed sea mats because they often form a covering over objects or surfaces. This is created by each individual animal making itself a protective case in which it lives.

 Bryozoans are filter feeders. They wave a crown of tiny tentacles in the water, which filter out water and catch microscopic morsels of food from the current.

 Some bryozoans start off as free-swimming larvae that move through the water. When a larva reaches a surface it can live on, it glues itself to that surface and grows a protective case.

Fact file

Lives: Northern Europe, North America

Habitat: Water

Size: Up to 1 mm long

Eats: Organic particles in water

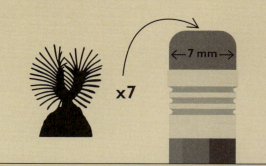

Bryozoans multiply by making exact copies, or clones, of themselves.

 In autumn, freshwater bryozoans make packets of reproductive cells called statoblasts. The adult animals die off while the statoblasts are dormant over winter. The larvae are released in spring to start new colonies.

Bedbug
Cimex lectularius

- Bedbugs hide in dark places in and around bedding, furniture, and even wallpaper. They come out at night to suck the blood of sleeping people.

- A bedbug needs to feed every few days, and finishes its meal within 10 minutes. A bedbug's bite is not usually noticed, but it might itch later.

- As it grows, a bedbug has to take at least one blood meal between molts. This is when it sheds its old skin to free its newer, larger body.

- With a good supply of food and in warm conditions, an adult female can lay up to five eggs a day, and up to 500 over a lifetime.

- Bedbug populations can double every 16 days in the right conditions.

- Some dogs have been trained to find bedbugs by smell to help manage infestations.

Fact file

Lives: Worldwide

Habitat: Dark, concealed spaces

Size: Up to 6 mm long

Eats: Blood of warm-blooded animals

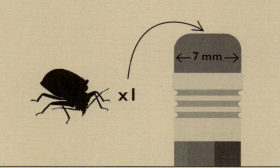

- Bedbugs are attracted to the carbon dioxide humans breathe out. They home in on body heat to find their meal.

- In ancient Rome, bedbugs were considered a good remedy for anyone bitten by a poisonous snake.

Chalcid wasp

Cirrospilus ingenuus

- These colorful, shiny wasps are parasites. Chalcid (*kal-sid*) wasps lay their eggs inside the bodies of other creatures, such as insects and spiders. The hatched wasp larva devours the host insect alive until the wasp has grown into an adult and is ready to leave. The host is left to die.

- This species of chalcid wasp attacks the larvae of citrus leafminers—moths that infest citrus trees. The wasp larva grows and feeds on the leafminer from the inside even after the leafminer turns into a pupa, its next stage of life.

- Many types of chalcid wasp are used as a pest control. The wasps lay their eggs in insect pests that attack crops, destroying the unwanted insects in the process of growing. The wasps' parasitic behavior keeps crops from disappearing under millions of caterpillars and stops flies from breeding out of control.

- While these wasps may be deadly to many insects, they do not sting.

Fact file

Lives: Asia, Australia, North Africa, North America

Habitat: Citrus trees

Size: 1.1–1.7 mm long

Eats: Citrus leafminers (as larva); nectar (as adult)

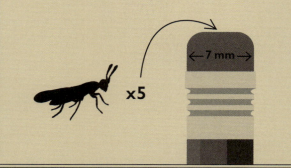

- There are thousands of types of chalcid wasp, all of them tiny. Most grow inside other insects' bodies, but some live in and eat seeds.

- A generation of chalcid wasp lasts a matter of weeks from egg to mature adult, depending on the temperature.

Peacock mite

Tuckerella japonica

- These mites are bright orange or red. They have white, leaf-shaped frills on their bodies called setae. The stiff setae might help the mites sense their surroundings.

- Despite their name, peacock mites do not live on peacocks. The name comes from the way the mites can suddenly flaunt their tail setae, in a similar way to how a peacock shows off its feathers.

- Peacock mites are found on plants, including tea bushes 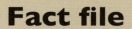 and citrus trees. The mites live in splits in the bark of young branches. Their bodies are flat so that they can easily slip into the small cracks.

- The long, thin setae at the tail end can be used like miniature whips to defend the mite against predators.

- To feed, a mite puts its sharp mouthpart into the wood of the plant or tree it is on. It injects spit to dissolve its food before sucking it up.

Fact file

Lives: Tropical tea-growing areas, particularly China, India, Sri Lanka, Kenya
Habitat: Tea bush bark
Size: 0.4 mm long
Eats: Young wood of tea bush

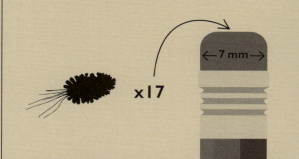

- The mite's eggs are about half the size of the female's body. They are laid in splits in the bark where the mites feed so the young can eat as soon as they hatch.

- Females stay near their eggs and young, and seem to protect them from small predators, such as other mites.

Weevil

Mecinus pascuorum

- A weevil is a small beetle with a long snout. There are nearly 100,000 known types of weevil.

- Many species of weevil are pests to humans. They infest stored dry foods such as wheat and rice, growing food such as maize, and cotton plants that we use to make clothes.

- This species of weevil is *Mecinus pascuorum*. It feeds on the plantain plant. The female lays an egg in part of the plantain plant, which contains two seeds. The larva feeds on the seeds as it grows into a pupa, then an adult weevil.

- The weevil's long rostrum, or snout, has chewing mouthparts. It uses these to munch tunnels into grains or other food.

Fact file

Lives: Europe, North America
Habitat: Grassland, scrubland
Size: Up to 6 mm long
Eats: Plantain

- Like other beetles, most weevils can fly. They have two sets of wings. The first set act as a hard case that covers the second set. When a weevil wants to fly, this first set opens out of the way to release the second set, which takes the creature into the air. This weevil's wings are folded on its back.

- Long ago, beetles similar to weevils were a problem for sailors because they infested the dry biscuits that were stored for long sea journeys. These biscuit weevils were not related to true weevils, but have given weevils a bad name!

Loriciferan

Nanaloricus mathildeae

- This strange sea creature has a tough outer case made of six plates. The armorlike covering is the lorica and is what gives the animal its name.

- The loriciferan is divided into a head, neck, thorax—its upper body—and abdomen, the lower body. The head ends in an opening for the mouth.

- This loriciferan species is *Nanaloricus mathildeae*. Not much is known about how it feeds, but scientists have seen it making a kind of leap—a brief backward movement followed by a sudden jump forward—perhaps toward food.

- There are many species of loriciferans, which all live between grains of sand and gravel on the seabed, though at different depths and in different conditions.

- These little creatures attach themselves firmly to the seafloor, making them difficult to find. Although they are thought to have existed for at least 500 million years, they were only discovered around 50 years ago.

- Loriciferan larvae go through several different body types before finally turning into adults. One type looks a lot like the adult, but with two "toes" at the back end of the body.

Fact file

Lives: Worldwide

Habitat: Sediment of the seabed

Size: 0.1–0.8 mm long

Eats: Bacteria, probably algae

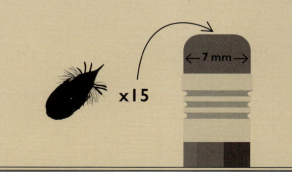

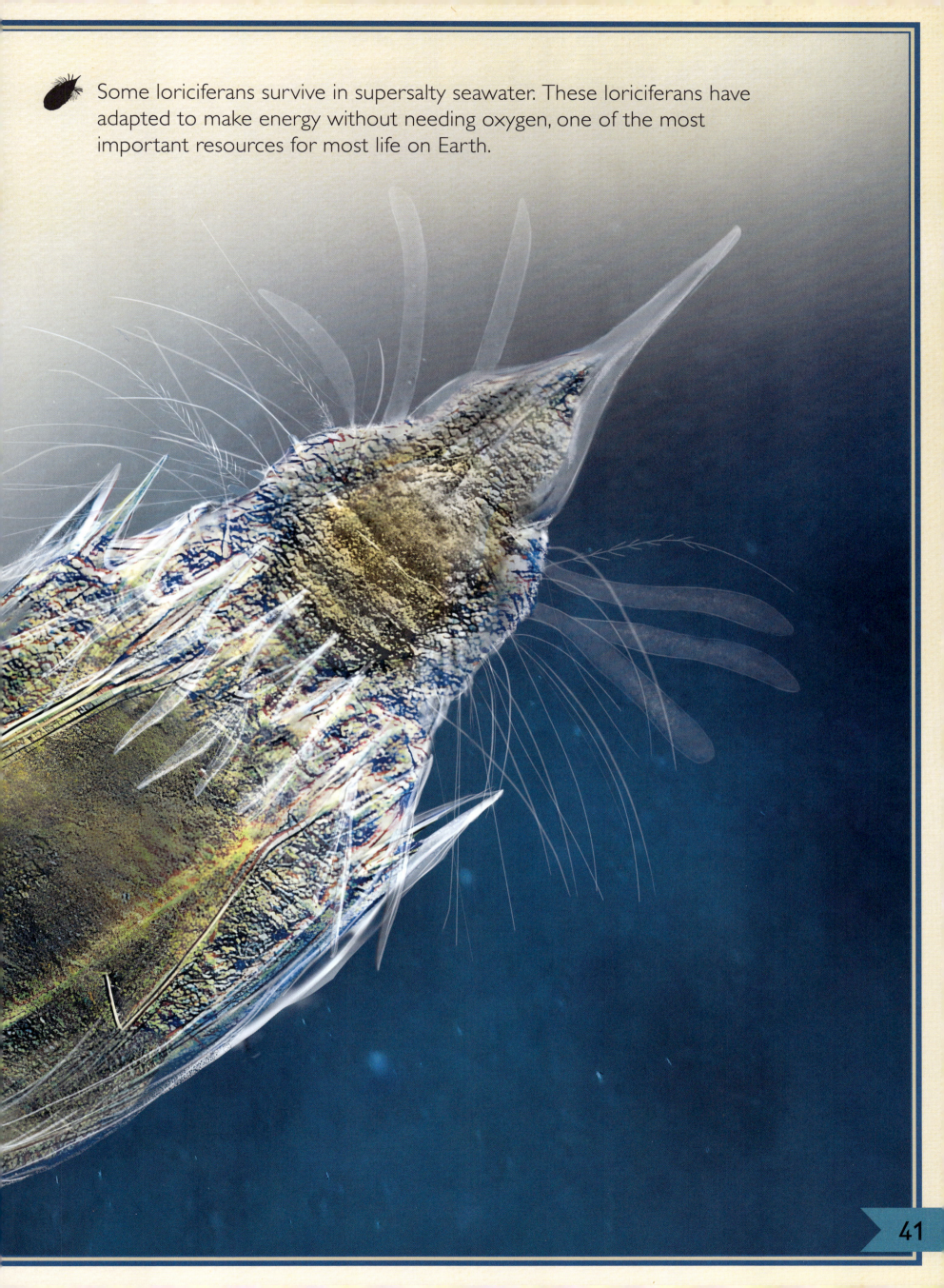

Some loriciferans survive in supersalty seawater. These loriciferans have adapted to make energy without needing oxygen, one of the most important resources for most life on Earth.

Hemispherical scale insect

Saissetia coffeae

- Check your plants for small lumps—they could be scale insects. These creatures are found on many plants, although it is often hard to tell they are animals at all. The tiny bugs sit motionless on a leaf or stem and feed on sap.

- Many scale insects spend all of their adult life feeding. Once they lodge themselves on a plant, with no limbs or head showing, they lose the use of their legs and never move from the spot again. Under the hard, shiny outer case, a long mouthpart pierces the plant's tissues to suck up sap.

- This scale insect is a hemispherical scale. These are all female and create offspring by making clones, or copies, of themselves.

- The insect lays hundreds of eggs in a space beneath her body. The nymphs that hatch, called crawlers, move to find a place to settle on a leaf or stem. This is the only stage of its life when the insect can move, although its legs are still present under the shield.

Fact file

Lives: Tropical and semitropical regions, hothouses

Habitat: Plant leaves, stems, and roots

Size: 2–4.5 mm long

Eats: Plant sap

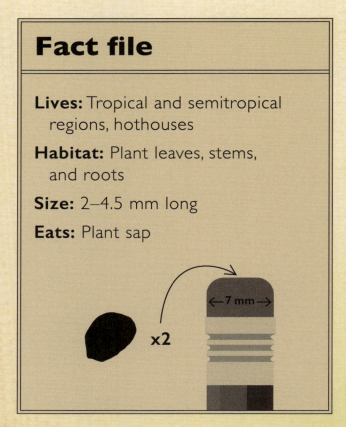

● Scale insects produce a sweet, sticky waste called honeydew. Some ants farm groups of scale insects so they can use the honeydew as a food supply. They herd crawlers toward good places to settle down, feed, and make the honeydew.

Follicular mite

Demodex folliculorum

- These mites usually live in follicles on people's faces. Follicles are where hairs grow from. The mites burrow into eyelash follicles and the glands, or groups of cells, that produce oils in the skin. Nearly everyone has at least some follicular mites.

- This mite feeds on an oily substance called sebum. Glands produce sebum to stop the skin drying out. Losing some sebum to hungry mites does no harm to the host.

- An adult human has around 5 million hair follicles on their body, which offer plenty of room for mites. They are mostly found on the cheeks, nose, eyelids, and forehead. A hair follicle can be home to a few mites. Each mite lives up against the hair shaft.

- Follicular mites live head down, with their front end buried in the follicle and the tail end sticking out.

- These mites live for about two weeks. They spend most of their time in hair follicles, but crawl out onto the skin at night in order to mate. They then return to the follicles to lay their eggs.

Fact file

Lives: Worldwide
Habitat: Human skin
Size: 0.1–0.2 mm long
Eats: Sebum

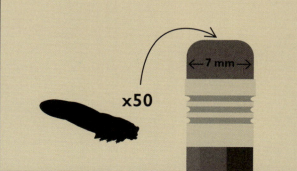

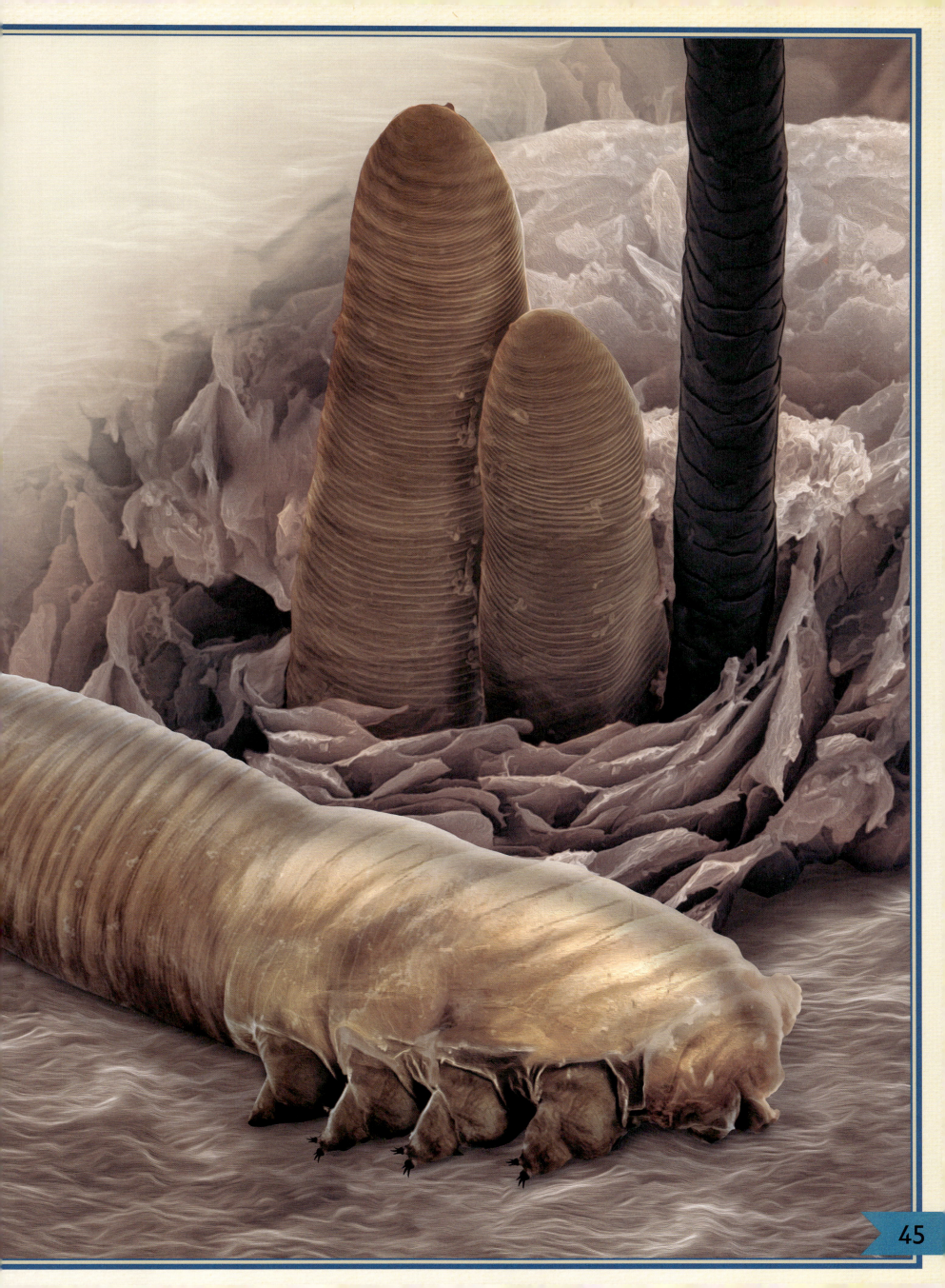

Slender herald snail

Carychium tridentatum

- This small, eyeless snail is usually less than 1/16 inch (2 mm) long—it is a tiny version of larger, more well-known snails. It is a type of micro snail, most of which live in water.

- The slender herald snail has a jagged mouthpart lined with small teeth called a radula. It shaves off particles of food to eat, a bit like a built-in cheese grater.

- Like all snails, the slender herald has great difficulty controlling water loss from its body. This is why it needs to stay damp. It retreats into its shell both for protection from danger and to avoid drying out.

- There is a limit to how small snails can be. The shell has to be large enough to contain the adult's body and at least one snail egg before it is laid. The baby snail must also be big enough to have enough nerve cells to function.

Fact file

Lives: Europe
Habitat: Leaf litter in woodland
Size: 1.8–2.3 mm high
Eats: Decaying plant matter

The smallest of all micro snails is even tinier than the slender herald, at less than half a millimeter long.

Needle midge

Contarinia pseudotsugae

- This needle midge is a tiny orange fly that spends its life in and around the Douglas fir pine tree.

- The female uses her ovipositor—a long tube at her back end for laying eggs—to probe into fir tree buds and among new leaves, known as needles. Here she lays her eggs, which are ready for hatching a few days later.

- When a needle midge egg hatches, the larva burrows into a newly growing needle. The midge feeds on the needle from the inside, causing it to become damaged and discolored. This creates a gall, or swelling, on the needle's underside.

- A needle midge larva feeds on the inside of a fir tree needle during the summer. When it is fully grown, it makes a triangular hole in the needle and drops to the ground.

Fact file

Lives: North America and western Europe

Habitat: Douglas fir tree forests

Size: 3 mm long

Eats: Douglas fir tree needles (as larvae)

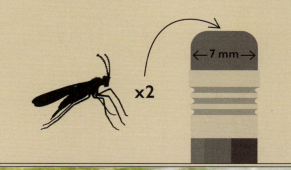

- Over winter, beneath the tree, the larva becomes a pupa, the next stage in its life cycle. In spring, it emerges as a fly and mates.

- Adult flies live only a few days. A male lives for up to two days and a female up to four days.

Flatworm

Gyratrix hermaphroditus

- All flatworms have a simple, soft body, with no internal organs except a gut. This flatworm is a type called *Gyratrix*.

- With no heart, lungs, or blood vessels, a flatworm cannot breathe in the same way as many larger creatures. Instead, oxygen passes directly through the surface of its flat, ribbonlike body, reaching all its cells. Carbon dioxide leaves the worm in the same way.

- *Gyratrix* is an unusual flatworm because it can live in almost any kind of water—saltwater, fresh water, or brackish water, which is a mix of salty and fresh water where a river meets the ocean.

- The worm uses the same opening both to eat and to eject waste. It must digest each meal fully before it can take in another.

- The flatworm has a pair of simple spots for eyes. These can sense light but do not see in the same way humans do.

- Some types of aquatic flatworm can regrow a whole body from cut-off pieces.

Fact file

Lives: Worldwide

Habitat: Fresh water and seawater

Size: 1–1.5 mm long

Eats: Microscopic water creatures, microalgae

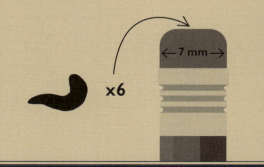

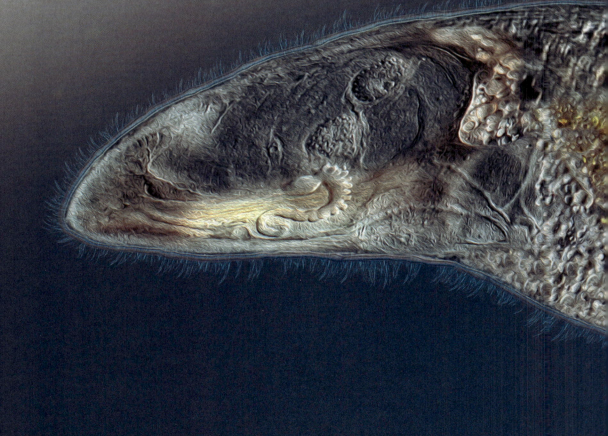

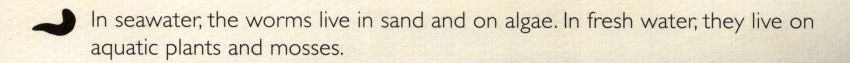 In seawater, the worms live in sand and on algae. In fresh water, they live on aquatic plants and mosses.

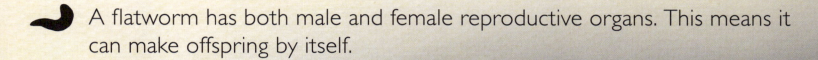 A flatworm has both male and female reproductive organs. This means it can make offspring by itself.

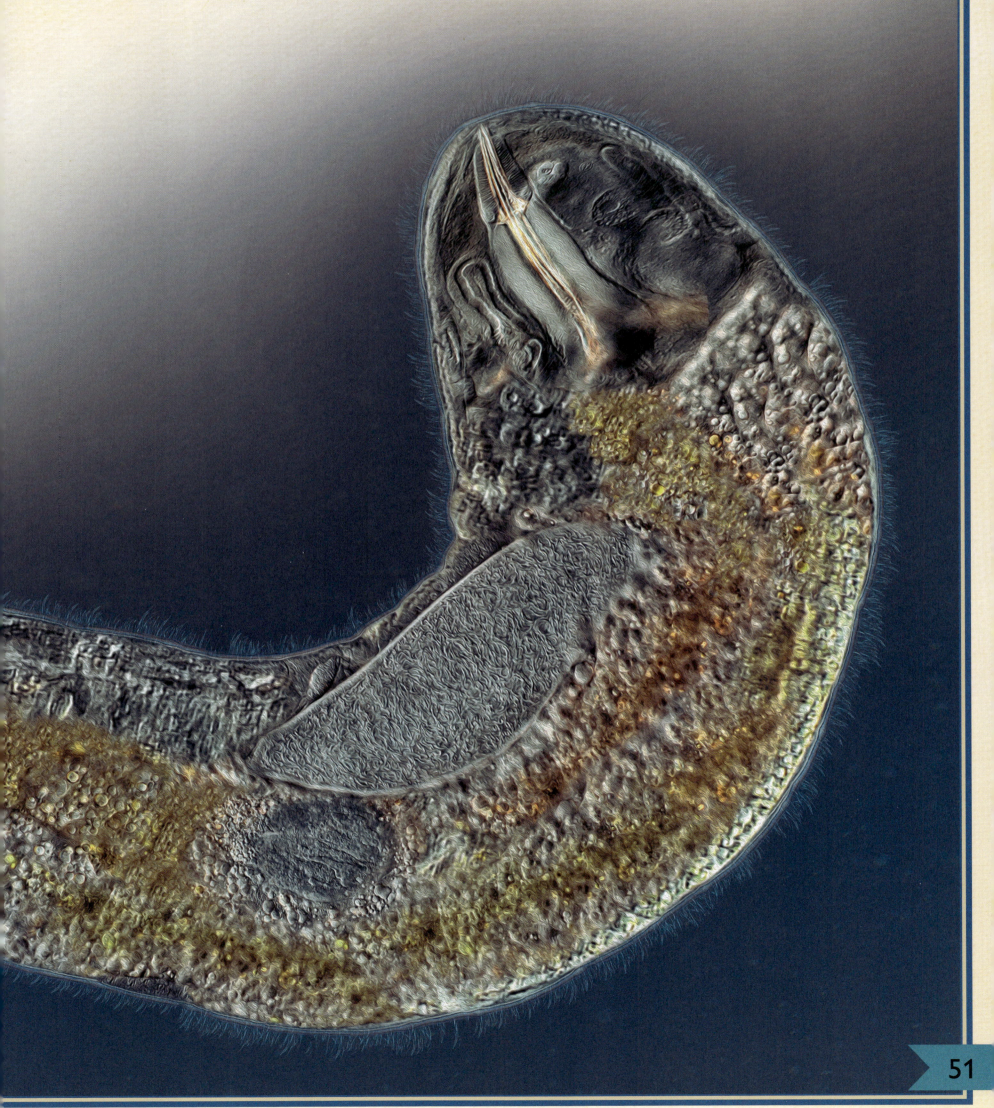

Oribatid mite

Liacarus subterraneus

- Oribatid mites live in the soil. Finding them is a sign that the soil is healthy. The mites depend on the nutrients in the soil to survive.

- These mites perform an important role in soil health. Their bodies break down the fungus, bacteria, and dead plant matter they eat, and return vital chemicals to the soil in their waste.

- *Liacarus* mites like this one have a hard, shiny, shell-like cuticle that protects their body. A special chemical makes the cuticle water-resistant—like a built-in raincoat!

- In forests, there can be up to half a million oribatid mites in each square yard (square meter) of soil.

- Each mite lives about two to seven years, depending on conditions in its habitat.

- The mite's cuticle keeps the creature clean and dry, protecting it from conditions found in the soil. It also stops the animal drying out—water cannot pass in or out through the cuticle.

Fact file

Lives: Worldwide
Habitat: Soil
Size: Up to 1.5 mm long
Eats: Fungus, bacteria

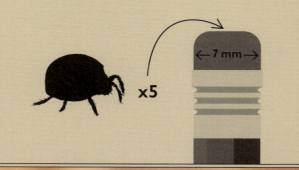

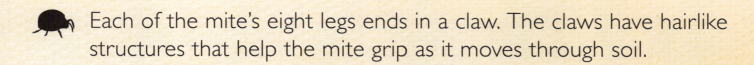 Each of the mite's eight legs ends in a claw. The claws have hairlike structures that help the mite grip as it moves through soil.

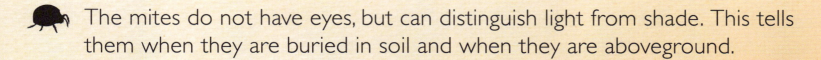 The mites do not have eyes, but can distinguish light from shade. This tells them when they are buried in soil and when they are aboveground.

Nematode

Caenorhabditis elegans

- This nematode worm is *Caenorhabditis elegans*. It lives in soil in temperate regions. These are warm but not tropical places.

- There are many types of nematode. They live all over the world, from the deepest ocean and far underground to the highest mountains and even deserts. Some live alone, in soil or water, while others are parasites that live inside other organisms.

- Nematodes are by far the most numerous animals on Earth. It is thought they make up to 80 percent of all living animals.

- Unlike the earthworms found in soil, nematodes' bodies are not made of segments. They have no respiratory or circulatory system. Instead, nematodes receive oxygen when gases pass straight through their skin.

- This nematode has see-through skin. Its intestine can be seen running nearly the entire length of its body.

Fact file

Lives: Worldwide

Habitat: Water, soil, other organisms

Size: 1 mm

Eats: Bacteria

Caenorhabditis elegans is an important creature for science. Studying its genetic material—the stuff that controls how living things function—and its 302 nerve cells has taught scientists a lot about how some animals develop.

Copepod

Cyclops sp.

- A copepod is a small crustacean with a hard shell. It is related to shrimps and crabs.

- This is a type of copepod called cyclops. It is named after the one-eyed monster from Greek mythology. The copepod's eye is red, but others can be black.

- Copepods are found in nearly all freshwater and saltwater habitats. This one lives in fresh water, where it swims with a sudden, jerky motion.

- Copepods, including cyclops species, are types of zooplankton. These are tiny animals that are fed on by many other water-based creatures. Zooplankton and phytoplankton, or plant plankton, are very important in the food chain because they are a vital food source for so many larger creatures.

- Females lay their eggs into pouches on either side of the body. They carry them around until the eggs hatch into larvae called nauplii. The nauplii have heads and tails with legs, but no main body segment. They develop into adults after a week.

- Cyclops have a clever way to escape predators. They unleash a sudden burst of energy for about a second that powers them far enough away from an attack.

Fact file

Lives: Worldwide

Habitat: Slow-moving or still fresh water

Size: 0.5–5 mm long

Eats: Algae, other plankton

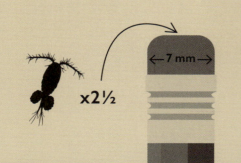

European red mite

Panonychus ulmi

 This is a spider mite. It is not a spider, but does belong to the same group of species. Its name comes from the ability to spin silk, a skill it shares with spiders.

 This mite is a female. The females are brick red and have white hairs on their backs. Females are slightly larger than the males, which are yellowy-red and have a slimmer body shape.

 These mites usually live and feed on the underside of fruit tree leaves. They move to the top side if the underneath becomes too crowded.

 Females live two to four weeks and produce hundreds of eggs in their lifetimes, laying up to 20 a day. These hatch in three days. Fertilized eggs always produce female mites. But spider mites can also lay eggs without mating, and these always produce males.

 In autumn, spider mites lay eggs on the bark of apple and other fruit trees to make sure they survive the winter. In summer, eggs are laid on the underside of leaves.

Fact file

Lives: Worldwide
Habitat: Fruit tree leaves
Size: 0.3–0.4 mm long
Eats: Leaves, stems of plants

🕷 The mites travel by spinning silken threads, which are left to be caught by the wind, carrying the mites between the trees.

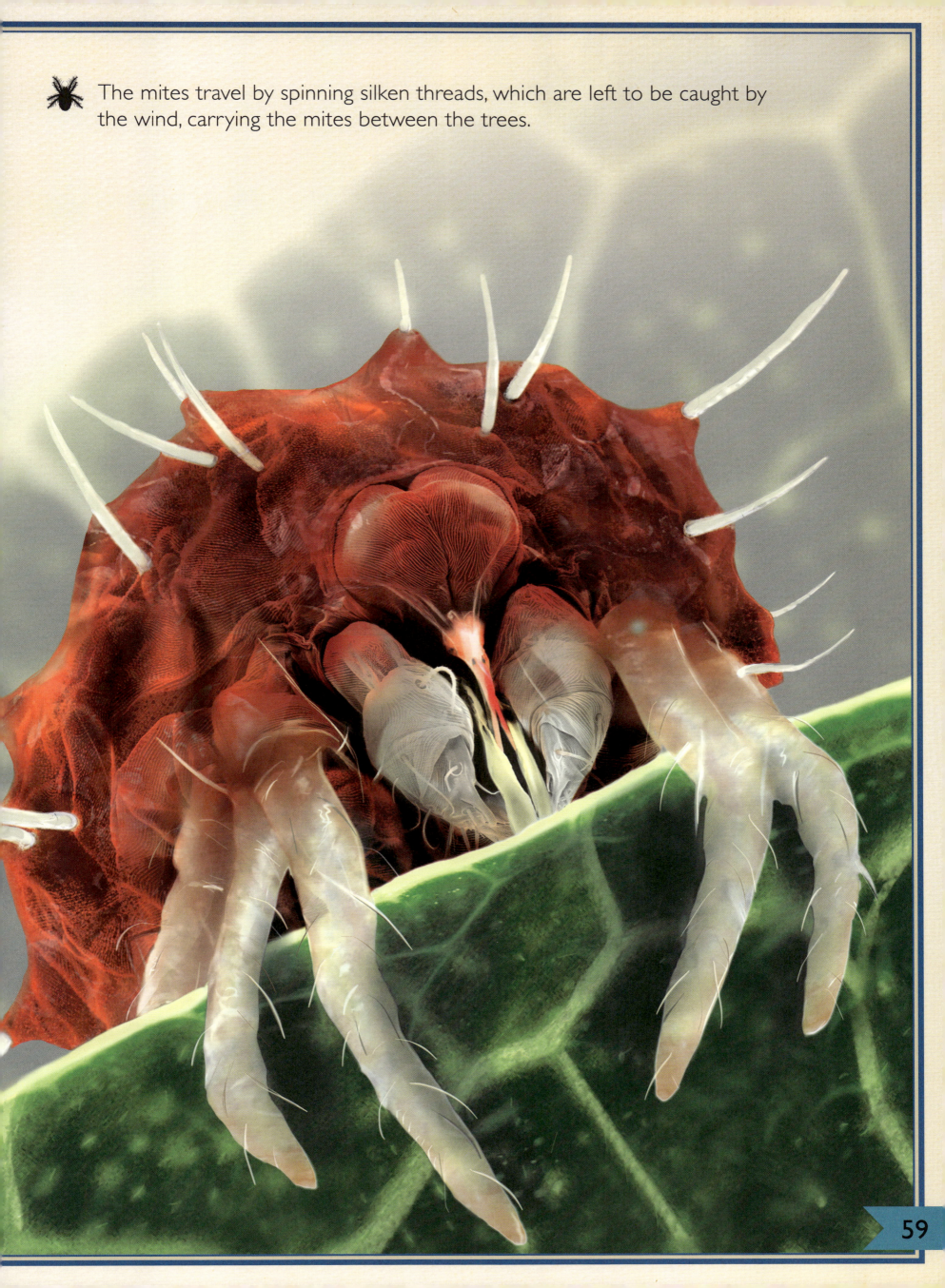

Pygmy sorrel moth

Enteucha acetosae

- Moths are winged insects that are often active at night. This moth is one of the smallest in the world. Its wingspan can be as tiny as 2.65 millimeters—about the width of a spaghetti strand.

- Like other moths, the pygmy sorrel has two pairs of wings covered with light scales. These are actually special types of hair. The moths also have feathery antennae, which are used to detect chemicals in the air for finding food or a mate. This moth's antennae are folded back beside its body.

- The female pygmy sorrel moth lays eggs on the underside of dock plant leaves and other types of sorrel. It can produce two or three generations of moth a year.

Fact file

Lives: Europe
Habitat: Sorrel plant leaves
Size: 3–4 mm wingspan
Eats: Sorrel leaves (as caterpillars)

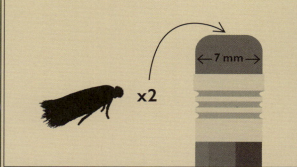

- Pygmy sorrel larvae are pale yellow caterpillars. They burrow between the top and bottom layers of sorrel leaves to feed on them. As the caterpillars eat, they create tiny channels that mark the leaves with thin, red, squiggly lines.

- The moth's larvae leave their sorrel plant burrows when it is time to pupate. They form a pupal case just 1/16 inch (1.5 mm) long. Pupae either emerge the following month in the summer, or the following spring if the eggs are laid later in the year.

Pharaoh ant

Monomorium pharaonis

- This yellow-brown ant lives in large colonies. It is often found in buildings and ships, where it can be very invasive because of its tiny size and large numbers.

- The pharaoh ant has been transported around the world with humans. This has allowed it to colonize areas it could not otherwise reach. It survives in colder areas by moving into warm buildings.

- Pharaoh ant colonies can live across several linked nests. The ants sometimes even move between them—they are fully functioning communities!

- Like other ants, pharaoh ants have different castes, or ranks. Each one has a particular role in the colony. Queens are the only breeding females. Other ants are nonbreeding female workers and winged males that mate with the queen.

Fact file

Lives: Worldwide

Habitat: In buildings worldwide; lives outside only in the tropics

Size: 2–3 mm long

Eats: Human food and food waste, dead animals, other insects

- Each ant colony can have several queens. This allows it to split easily, producing new colonies, each one with a queen.

- Pharaoh ants make different types of chemical trails. One type marks a route to a good food source and is attractive to the ants, making them more likely to follow it. Another is an off-putting trail that marks a lack of food.

Scabies mite

Sarcoptes scabiei

- The scabies mite is a parasite, a living thing that lives on another living thing. This mite causes the disease scabies in humans. It is found in the top layer of an infested person's skin and causes a very itchy rash.

- The mites' front legs have long, suckerlike ends, which allow them to hold onto their host's skin.

- Female mites make a burrow in the outer layer of a host's skin to lay their eggs. They lay two to three eggs each day for the rest of their lives, which are up to two months long.

- The folded surface of the mite's body is covered with spines and bristles. They provide grip as it moves through a host's skin.

- Scabies mite eggs hatch in three to four days. The hatched larvae crawl out onto the skin and look for somewhere to make a molting pouch, or burrow, and grow into adults.

- These mites create burrows using their mouthparts and special cutting surfaces on the front legs.

Fact file

Lives: Worldwide, especially crowded tropical areas
Habitat: Human body
Size: Females 0.3–0.45 mm long
Eats: Skin

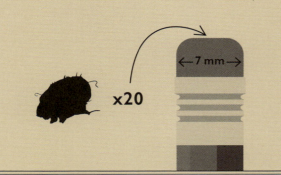

Male mites are smaller than females and rarely seen. They make shallow pits in the skin to feed until they can find a female's burrow and mate.

Fruit fly

Drosophila melanogaster

- Tiny fruit flies like this one arrive silently to feast on unripe or rotting fruit left out on a warm day.

- Like many insects, the life cycle of a fruit fly has four stages—egg, larva, pupa, and adult. It takes eight to 12 days for the fly to develop from an egg to an adult. Their whole life cycle lasts up to 50 days.

- Female fruit flies are very fertile and can lay up to 100 eggs a day. This means a fly population grows very quickly.

- The fly has compound eyes. Each eye is made up of many small lenses that work together to let it see. Humans have only one lens per eye.

- A fruit fly's body is covered in tiny bristles that help it sense movement in its environment. Its antennae are also sensitive—they can detect sound, wind movement, and gravity.

Fact file

Lives: Worldwide

Habitat: Near fruit and rotting food, including in homes

Size: 2–4 mm long

Eats: Fruit

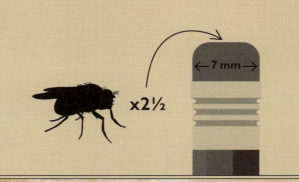

x2½ ←7 mm→

Fruit flies are important to science because they can be used to study how characteristics are passed down from one generation to the next. This is because the flies have a very short life cycle, meaning lots of generations can be studied at the same time, and are easy to look after.

Bdelloid rotifer

Adineta tuberculosis

- This strange creature is a bdelloid (*dell-oid*) rotifer. These animals live in watery environments all around the world, including in damp soil and vegetation. Most live in fresh water, but a few are found in seawater.

- Rotifers are made up of a head at one end, a body and gut in the middle, and a single foot at the other end. They are partly see-through, meaning their insides and even some of what they have eaten are visible.

- All bdelloid rotifers are female. They reproduce by making clones, or exact copies, of themselves from an unfertilized egg.

- These creatures are very hardy. While all life needs water to exist, rotifers can survive their bodies being completely dehydrated, or dried out, before being rehydrated. They can also survive low oxygen, starvation, and very acidic conditions.

- Bdelloid rotifers have a special ability. They can absorb genes from bacteria, fungi, and plants. Genes are the codes living things need to function and develop. Up to a tenth of a bdelloid rotifer's genes may be from other species!

There are many different types of rotifer. A drop in the population of certain species can indicate water pollution. Scientists can monitor them to keep checks on environmental conditions.

Bdelloid rotifers can withstand very high amounts of radiation. This makes some scientists think they could even survive in space.

Fact file

Lives: Worldwide
Habitat: Fresh water, wet soil, damp moss, seawater
Size: 0.2–0.5 mm long
Eats: Decaying organic matter, algae

x20
← 7 mm →

Cat flea

Ctenocephalides felis

- These fleas feed on the blood of domestic cats and dogs. They suck up the blood using a proboscis, a sharp tube that they insert into a host's skin.

- Fleas can jump great distances. On average, they can spring 8 inches (20 cm)—that's about 66 times their body length.

- Cat fleas are so thin that they appear nearly flat when viewed head-on. This makes it easier for them to slide through the thick fur of a cat host. They use their strong claws to grip onto hairs.

- The fleas' bodies carry a number of backward-facing bristles. As a cat grooms itself, the bristles become caught on the animal's hair, trapping the fleas in its fur and making sure they are not brushed away. The direction of the bristles also means the fleas can only move forward through their host's fur.

- A female can produce 20 to 50 eggs a day—that adds up to hundreds over her lifetime. Eggs are slippery and fall off the animal to develop elsewhere.

- Flea larvae live in dark places, such as in carpet fibers. They feed on the poop of adult fleas and flea eggs that have fallen off the host animal.

Fact file

Lives: Worldwide
Habitat: Cat and dog fur
Size: 1–2 mm long
Eats: Blood

A flea larva forms a pupa and later emerges as an adult. It then needs a host. It finds one by sensing a cat's body heat and the carbon dioxide it exhales. The flea leaps on and begins to feed.

Head shield slug

Colpodaspis thompsoni

- This colorful animal is a type of sea slug. Like a snail, it carries a coiled shell on its back, but it is hidden underneath its soft, slippery mantle, or body, making it look like it is inflated like a bubble. This is why the slug is also known as a bubble snail.

- The head shield slug's thin shell makes a bulge in the middle of the mantle, where it protects the internal organs.

- Head shield slugs have both male and female reproductive parts. This means they can mate with any other slug of their species. They lay long strings of eggs.

Fact file

Lives: Tropical and semitropical seas

Habitat: Rocks and coral

Size: 2–3 mm long

Eats: Unknown

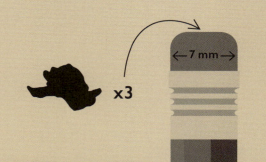

- The slug has two eyes. They are slightly sunken into the skin, just in front of the shell.

- Under the slug's foot, a special mucus organ makes a slime that helps the animal to stick to the algae-covered rocks that it slides over.

- Two tentacles on its head allow the animal to taste the water. Perhaps this is to help it find food or a mate.

Ostracod

Tanycypris centa

- Ostracods are sometimes called seed shrimps, because they are so small they look like seeds. They live in many places, including the sea, lakes, rivers, ponds, and rice fields. This one, *Tanycypris centa*, lives in fresh water.

- These creatures swim using their two pairs of antennae. The antennae are covered in tiny bristles, which helps the ostracod drag itself through the water.

- The ostracod has a carapace, or shell, which can be closed to protect the rest of its body. The shell is divided into two halves that are connected by a hinge, rather like a clamshell. One half of the shell is on the right side of the animal and one on the left, with the hinge running along the middle of its back.

- Some ostracod species have a special trick. If threatened by a predator, they can escape by jumping through the water using two spiky limbs at the tail end. When the limbs uncoil, they push the ostracod upward and away.

Fact file

Lives: Asia
Habitat: Fresh water
Size: 1 mm long
Eats: Tiny organic remains, algae

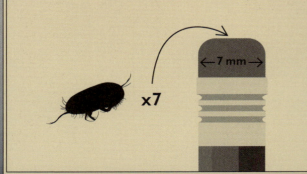

- All *Tanycypris centa* specimens found have been female. Scientists think this means they probably reproduce without a male by cloning themselves. This is the same for many freshwater ostracod species.

- Many freshwater ostracods live in pools that dry up for part of the year. Females lay resting eggs, which only develop and hatch when the water returns and the young can survive.

Red velvet mite

Trombidium sp.

- This mite is called the red velvet mite because its body is covered with lots of tiny hairs, which look like red velvet.

- There are many types of velvet mite. Most are small, but some giant varieties in India and Africa grow to almost half an inch (more than 1 cm) long.

- The mites live in the soil and in leaf litter. They come out after rain to search for insects, spiders, and spider eggs to feed on.

- Velvet mite larvae are parasites. They live on other arthropods—animals with external skeletons—and eat by sucking their host's body fluids. The larvae drop off their hosts to dig into the soil and change form as they grow.

- Female red velvet mites lay hundreds of eggs at a time during spring and early summer. The eggs only develop and hatch in warm, humid conditions, as humidity is vital to their development.

- Like other mites, velvet mites are related to spiders. They have eight legs as adults, but only have six as larvae.

Fact file

Lives: Worldwide

Habitat: Soil and leaf litter

Size: Up to 4 mm long

Eats: Larger arthropods such as beetles, spiders, termites

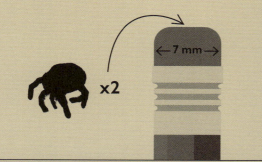

In very hot, cold, or dry conditions, these mites can hibernate and wait for their preferred warm, humid conditions in which they can easily hunt for food.

Water flea

Daphnia magna

- Water fleas are see-through—their eggs and internal organs are visible through their bodies.

- This type of water flea is *Daphnia magna*. It is a typical water flea species, and has a carapace, or hard outside, five pairs of legs, and a single eye.

- The flea is a filter feeder, eating algae and tiny bits of plant matter that are floating in the water. The creature moves its leaf-shaped legs to push currents of water around itself. This allows it to funnel food particles toward its mouth.

- Female water fleas usually reproduce alone. The offspring are female clones of the mother, but fleas can also produce males. Eggs are kept in a special brooding chamber under the carapace. They hatch after a day and the young develop in the chamber for three more days.

- *Daphnia magna* lays up to 100 eggs every three to four days for around two months.

Fact file

Lives: Northern hemisphere
Habitat: Still, fresh water
Size: Up to 5 mm long
Eats: Algae, bacteria, dead plant matter

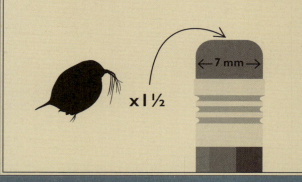

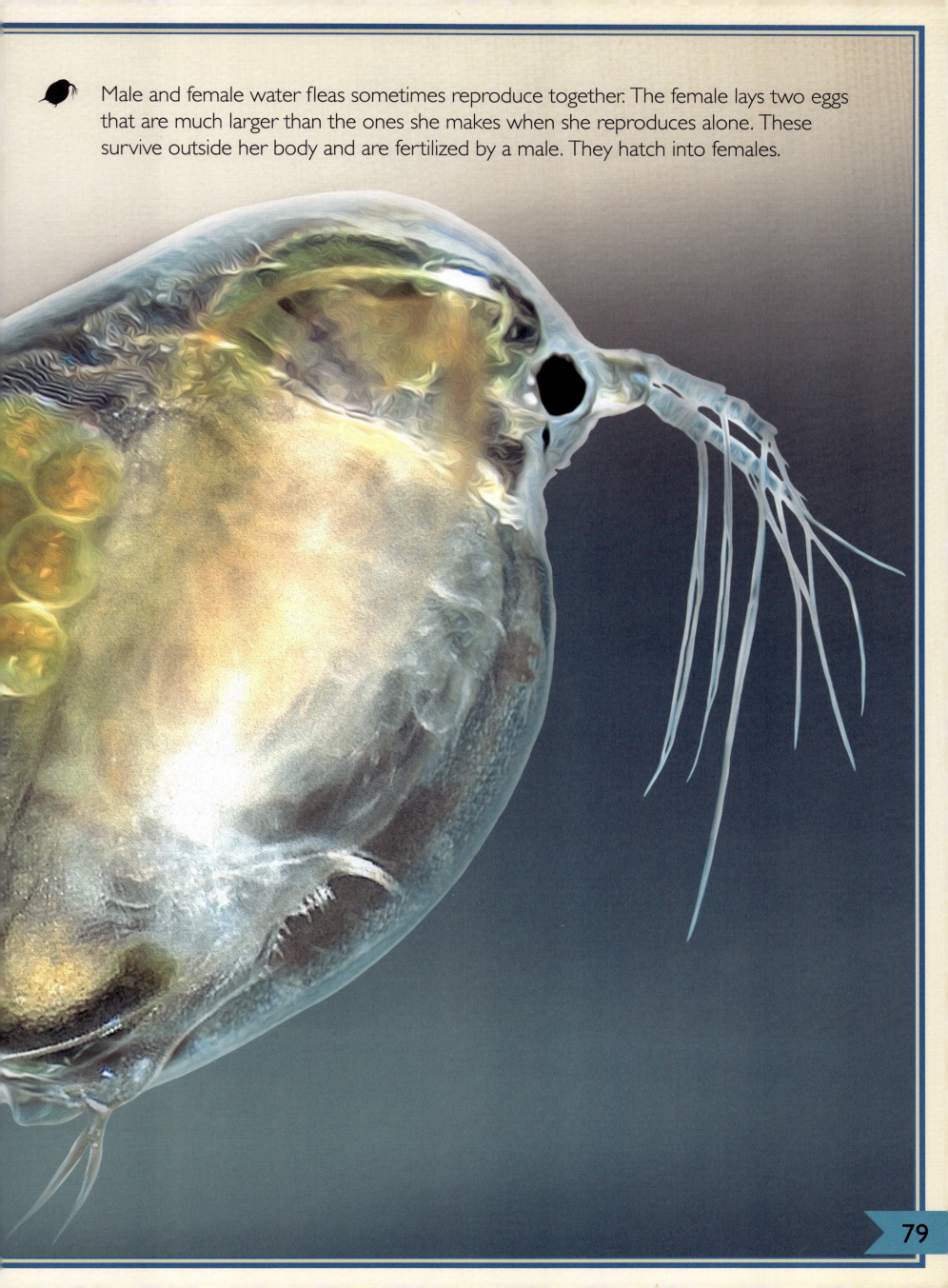

Male and female water fleas sometimes reproduce together. The female lays two eggs that are much larger than the ones she makes when she reproduces alone. These survive outside her body and are fertilized by a male. They hatch into females.

Microscopic creatures

1 mm scale

1 cm scale

- Follicular mite 0.1–0.2 mm
- Dust mite 0.1–0.4 mm
- Bdelloid rotifer 0.2–0.5 mm
- European red mite 0.3–0.4 mm
- Scabies mite 0.3–0.45 mm
- Peacock mite 0.4 mm
- Loriciferan 0.1–0.8 mm
- Tardigrade 0.5 mm
- Mud dragon 1 mm
- Bryozoan 1 mm
- Nematode 1 mm
- Ostracod 1 mm

- Flatworm 1–1.5 mm
- Chalcid wasp 1.1–1.7 mm
- Cat flea 1–2 mm
- Oribatid mite 1.5 mm
- Springtail 0.2–3 mm
- Varroa mite 1.8 mm
- Black bean aphid 1–3 mm
- Slender herald snail 1.8–2.3 mm
- Head louse 2–3 mm
- Pharaoh ant 2–3 mm
- Tanaid 2–3 mm
- Head shield slug 2–3 mm

- Fruit fly 2–4 mm
- Sheep tick 2.4–3.6 mm
- Needle midge 3 mm
- Copepod 0.5–5 mm
- Hemispherical scale insect 2–4.5 mm
- Pygmy sorrel moth 3–4 mm
- Red velvet mite 4 mm

- Water flea 5 mm
- Polychaete 5 mm
- Pseudoscorpion 2–8 mm
- Weevil 6 mm
- Bedbug 6 mm